# SOUTH COAST PASSENGER VESSELS

John Megoran

*Front Cover*: *Wight Scene*.

*Back Cover*: *Maid of the Islands* off Brownsea.

First published 2019

Amberley Publishing
The Hill, Stroud
Gloucestershire, GL5 4EP

www.amberley-books.com

Copyright © John Megoran, 2019

The right of John Megoran to be identified as the Author of this work has been asserted in accordance with the Copyrights, Designs and Patents Act 1988.

All rights reserved. No part of this book may be reprinted or reproduced or utilised in any form or by any electronic, mechanical or other means, now known or hereafter invented, including photocopying and recording, or in any information storage or retrieval system, without the permission in writing from the Publishers.

British Library Cataloguing in Publication Data.
A catalogue record for this book is available from the British Library.

ISBN 978 1 4456 8856 5 (print)
ISBN 978 1 4456 8857 2 (ebook)

Typeset in 10pt on 13pt Sabon.
Origination by Amberley Publishing.
Printed in the UK.

# Contents

|  | Introduction | 4 |
|---|---|---|
| Chapter 1 | Weymouth and Portland | 5 |
| Chapter 2 | Poole and Swanage | 9 |
| Chapter 3 | Christchurch | 21 |
| Chapter 4 | Western Solent | 26 |
| Chapter 5 | Southampton, Cowes and Portsmouth | 31 |
| Chapter 6 | West Sussex | 43 |
| Chapter 7 | Isle of Wight Ferries | 51 |
| Chapter 8 | Cross-Channel Ferries | 69 |
| Chapter 9 | Operational Preserved Steamships | 81 |
|  | Vessels that can Carry more than Twelve Passengers | 93 |
|  | Acknowledgements | 96 |

# Introduction

The south coast passenger vessel scene has changed so much in my lifetime. When I was a boy, the paddle steamers *Consul, Embassy, Monarch* and *Princess Elizabeth* were still plying their trade. All are now long gone, but a rough count tots up over eighty vessels with Maritime and Coastguard Agency Passenger Certificates still in service today in an area bounded by Weymouth in the west and Newhaven in the east, which forms the subject of this book. That's quite a lot of boats and quite a lot of boat trip options.

Many of these boats are comparatively small, with quite a number based on the formula of carrying 100/250 passengers with an enclosed deck with windows, so that passengers can see out, plus a top deck to experience the sun and the breeze on finer days. These sorts of boats are all under the command of boatmasters, rather than seagoing captains, and have very small crews of between two and four, making them very economical to operate.

At the other end of the spectrum, and for any who think that size matters, then the Isle of Wight and cross-Channel ferries have grown very much larger. The old Portsmouth to Fishbourne car ferry *Hilsea*, built in 1930, was just 149 GRT. The latest Wightlink ship on the same route, *Victoria of Wight*, is 8,041 GRT, which makes her fifty-four times larger than her diminutive predecessor.

The same is true of cross-Channel ferries. The *Falaise*, built in 1947 for the Southampton to St Malo service, was 3,700 GRT. *Bretagne*, which runs from Portsmouth to St Malo for Brittany Ferries today, is 24,534 GRT, making her nearly seven times bigger. Next year Brittany Ferries will take delivery of their latest ship, *Honfleur*, which will be 42,000 GRT.

Whether you like your boat trips on small craft, giant ferries or something in-between, then there is still a vibrant passenger vessel industry along the south coast today. The choice is large, ranging from day trips to France or the Channel Islands, to cruises to view parts of the coast, around harbours, up and down rivers, or along a canal.

I hope that this book encourages you to seek them all out and take as many trips as you can to enjoy the real pleasure of getting afloat in this beautiful part of Britain.

# Chapter 1

# Weymouth and Portland

Weymouth has a long history as an epicentre of passenger vessel operations. It was the base for Cosens & Company (paddle steamer operators), so from the middle of the nineteenth century right up to the 1960s the harbour was full of paddle steamers laid up for the winter, being refurbished for the summer season and then operating trips from the Pleasure Pier around the warships in Portland Harbour to Portland Bill, the Shambles Lightship, Lulworth Cove, Swanage and Bournemouth, Totland Bay and the Isle of Wight. Before the Second World War, trips were also taken westwards down the Devon coast to Torquay and Dartmouth, often calling at the harbours and beaches along the way, including at West Bay, Lyme Regis, Seaton, Sidmouth, Budleigh Salterton, Exmouth and Teignmouth.

In their heyday the railway-owned Channel Island mailboats also offered excursions from Weymouth along the Dorset coast in-between their cross-Channel work, as well as taking holidaymakers and locals alike on daytrips to the Channel Islands.

Then there were the fleets of small motor launches, which from the 1920s ran from two sets of pontoons on Weymouth Beach, taking people on trips around Portland Harbour. There was also a plethora of small twelve-seater passenger boats that collected their cargos from Weymouth's ferry steps. Speedboats were also available to take their charges on thrilling high-speed circuits of the bay.

Today almost all of that has gone and all that remains are the twelve-seaters, a speedboat, a back-crunching rib that bangs its passengers out to sea in search of big waves and fairground screams, and two of the former fifty-passenger beach boats, *My Girl* and *Enchantress*, which now run from inside the harbour from steps close to Brewers Quay.

What is really missing from Weymouth is the sort of 100/250-passenger vessel now common at Poole and in the Solent, which give passengers a more comfortable ride around Portland Harbour and down Dorset's beautiful Jurassic Coast to the marvel that is Lulworth Cove. However, there is a problem here. With their long history, the twelve-seaters dominate the market, and even half a dozen of them can put seventy-two passengers afloat at any one time. A dozen can service 144, which consistently picks off enough of the market to make a single larger passenger vessel lose its potential for profitability. Each of them is one-man owned and they sail with a crew of just one and have minimal operating costs. How does a larger passenger vessel with full MCA passenger certificates, and all the substantial expenses that go with it, compete?

However, let's keep cheerful and remember that there are two passenger vessels with MCA passenger certificates still operating from Weymouth. They are a delight and are rich in history.

*My Girl* was built in 1931 for excursions from Plymouth up the rivers Tamar and Yealm for the Hill family. Requisitioned for Royal Army Service Corp work in the Second World War, she was brought to Weymouth by brothers Ron and Bert Hill and spent her time ferrying troops out to the Portland breakwaters along with stores and ammunition for the harbour defences. In wartime her passenger capacity was upped to 100 and regular cargoes included fifty shells, each weighing a hundredweight apiece, along with 500 gallons of paraffin in 5-gallon cans for the searchlight generators.

After the war Ron Hill ran *My Girl* from pontoons towed round from Weymouth Harbour every day and positioned on the Weymouth Beach near the pier bandstand. It was a lucrative trade when the weather was fine and the wind wasn't blowing from the east, with Weymouth Beach in the 1950s and '60s being stuffed to bursting with holidaymakers mostly from the industrial hinterland of south Wales and the Midlands.

*Enchantress* was built in Canada in 1943 for the Royal Navy before being shipped to Weymouth, where she has remained ever since. Like *My Girl*, she helped to service the Portland breakwaters and acted as a liberty boat for ships at anchor in the war. Her hull was specially strengthened for working with cables and chains and it is thought that she was also involved with the deployment of barrage balloons. After the war she too found a new career working in tandem with *My Girl*, running from the beach pontoons.

Today the two boats offer trips out into the bay to view Ringstead, Osmington and White Nothe, as well as running a ferry service from Weymouth to Portland, calling at

*My Girl*.

Castletown and at the new Portland Marina. In this they are reviving a blast from the past as Cosens' paddle steamers operated a Weymouth to Portland ferry service from the middle of the nineteenth century, both before and after the coming of the railway. The arrival of the motor coach in the 1920s dented that trade, but the final Weymouth to Portland paddle steamer connection remained as late as the summer of 1965, when the paddle steamer *Princess Elizabeth* ferried passengers across to Castletown for Navy Days.

Weymouth has one other passenger boat service, and it is most unusual – a ferry across the harbour connecting the end of the esplanade with the Nothe. This is run by eight-seater rowing boats, with the oarsmen traditionally being ancient mariners who have doubtless spent a lifetime on craft with engines, but who now find themselves having to provide their own motive power.

*Enchantress.*

Aboard *My Girl* leaving Portland Harbour through the North Ship Channel.

One of Weymouth's numerous twelve-seater boats.

Weymouth's thrill-seeking, high-speed RIB.

Weymouth's rowing boat ferry.

# Chapter 2

# Poole and Swanage

The huge gap in this section is Bournemouth, once the doyen of south coast passenger vessel piers. In its heyday the pier was served by many paddle steamers with some based locally at Poole and others visiting on a daily basis from Weymouth, Southampton, Portsmouth and sometimes as far afield as Brighton. The trip options were many, from local rides across to Swanage or to Totland Bay and Yarmouth on the Isle of Wight, through to day excursions around the Isle of Wight, to Weymouth and, before the Second World War, as far afield as Dartmouth, the Channel Islands and Cherbourg.

Today Bournemouth Pier is still there but unfortunately there are no trip options. The local authority has not invested in maintenance of the landing stages, which are now falling down, and worse, work to pump millions of tons of sand from offshore onto Bournemouth Beach has reduced the depths alongside the pier to make it largely unserviceable. Before this work started there was a good 15 feet of water either side at chart datum – enough to float any local passenger vessel in at all states of the tide. Today there is less than 6 feet. At low water springs children can walk out from the beach alongside the decrepit landing stages.

However, the story is quite different just down the road at Poole, where passenger boat trips are doing rather well. A gigantic ria, Poole Harbour is one of the world's largest natural harbours and provides an oasis for boat trips as the sheltered conditions enable services to operate in pretty much any weather conditions. And to add to that the harbour is very scenic. It has the magical Brownsea Island, now owned by the National Trust, at its heart and it extends inland through delightful reed banks as far as Wareham.

The two largest operators are Brownsea Island Ferries and Greenslade Pleasure Boats. Although they are separate companies they do work together and between them can field seven boats – *Maid of Poole, Maid of the Harbour, Maid of the Islands, Maid of the Lakelands, Purbeck Gem, Purbeck Pride* and *Purbeck Princess* – with a combined passenger capacity of over a thousand at any one time. They run two main trips: one from Poole Quay to Brownsea Island, sailing out to the north of the island and, when the tide permits, returning to the south so as to give a complete circuit; and the other is from Sandbanks to Brownsea. In addition they run some excursions with their smaller boats upriver to Wareham. Occasionally they go further out for Jurassic Coast cruises towards St Alban's Head. Some of the boats have passenger certificates that extend to the Isle of Wight, although such trips are not in the regular schedule.

All their vessels were purpose built for these routes and are comparatively new, having entered service between 1989 and 2001. The two largest ones, *Maid of Poole* and *Maid of the Harbour*, have a seagoing feel about them with their sturdy bows and watertight foredeck doors.

Two other small launches carry passengers to Brownsea. *Castello* is owned by John Lewis and is used to transport their staff and guests to their training facility on the island, while *Brownsea Enterprise*, which is owned by the National Trust, is used as a ferry for their staff.

City Cruises run the *Solent Scene* and the *Island Scene* from Poole Quay, with the former making a couple of round trips every day to and from Swanage. This is a lovely cruise that is highly recommended, with it passing through not only the beauties of Poole Harbour and Sandbanks, but also extending out to sea and onwards past the Old Harry Rocks and into delightful Swanage Bay. The *Island Scene* offers short cruises from Poole Quay down to the harbour entrance, coming back to the south of Brownsea when the tides permit.

*Dorset Queen* carries passengers mostly on private charters. Built in 1938 as the *Gay Queen*, she originally ran from Rothesay on trips through the Kyles of Bute. Bought by Greenslades in the early 1990s, she had a brief sojourn at Falmouth as the *Queen of the Fal* from 2005 before taking up her current role at Poole in 2008. *Dorset Queen* has a luxurious feel about her, with varnish you could use as a mirror for combing your hair in.

At Wareham there is a small ex-Admiralty whaler called *Orca*, which offers 40-minute trips along the River Frome.

The Marsh family have run short boat trips from the Stone Quay at Swanage for 100 years and continue to do so today with their twelve-seater launch *Precious*.

Last but not least is the chain ferry *Bramble Bush Bay*. She hauls herself across the harbour entrance each day, connecting Sandbanks with Shell Bay and knocking miles off the more circuitous road route to Swanage via Wareham. She is worth riding on if only to take in the lovely scenery, with views up the harbour and across Poole Bay to the Needles.

*Maid of Poole* at Poole.

*Maid of Poole*'s seagoing bow.

*Maid of Poole* preparing to load passengers for Brownsea Island.

*Made of the Lakelands* passing Stakes buoy in Poole Harbour.

*Maid of the Islands* leaving Sandbanks.

*Maid of the Islands* with Brownsea beyond.

The top deck of *Maid of Poole*.

*Maid of Poole* proceeding down the Middle Ship Channel in Poole Harbour.

*Maid of Poole* alongside at Brownsea Island.

*Maid of Poole*'s saloon.

*Purbeck Princess* alongside at Poole.

*Purbeck Princess* loading for Brownsea.

*Purbeck Princess* setting off for Brownsea.

*Purbeck Pride* arriving at Poole.

*Purbeck Gem* at Poole.

*Solent Scene* leaving Poole.

*Solent Scene* arriving at Swanage Pier.

*Island Scene* at Poole.

*Island Scene* passing Sandbanks.

*Castello* with Lilliput in the background.

*Castello* alongside at Brownsea Island.

*Brownsea Enterprise* leaving Sandbanks.

*Brownsea Enterprise* alongside at Brownsea Island.

*Dorset Queen* at Poole.

*Dorset Queen* with her immaculate varnish.

*Orca* at Wareham.

*Precious* at Swanage.

The Sandbanks/Shell Bay chain ferry *Bramble Bush Bay*.

# Chapter 3

# Christchurch

If you like your boat rides on flat calms without any of the rocking and rolling that going to sea can sometimes entail, then take a trip on one of the delightful little boats that run to the mouth of Christchurch Harbour from near the road bridge at Tuckton Tea Gardens. Built in the 1930s and still in original condition, *Headland Belle*, *Headland Maid*, *Headland Pal* and *Headland Queen* carry up to fifty passengers each on trips back into a bygone era as they meander their quiet way down the narrow River Stour, calling at Wick Ferry, Christchurch Quay and then on as the river opens out to land at Mudeford Beach. Built of wood, there is much use of varnish. They are how small passenger boats used to be before the Second World War.

As the harbour is very shallow at low tide, each of the boats has a tiny draft even when fully loaded. To protect their propellers from weed and catching on the bottom, the propellers are located in a tunnel inside the hulls, with water drawn in ahead of the propeller and pushed out through the stern. It is an unusual arrangement and it gives them unusual handling characteristics.

At the first stop after Tuckton Tea Gardens you can get off and cross on the Wick Ferry, which is an open boat carrying just twelve. There are those who say that this ferry was founded before the building of Christchurch Priory, which would give it a 1,000-year history. Whether or not that is true, it is quite certain that there has been a Wick Ferry throughout the last 200 years. It is not a very long crossing, taking only a few minutes. It runs every day in the summer if the weather is fine and you can tell that it is working, as on many other similar small ferries, by whether or not the flag is flying from the landing stage.

Down near the harbour mouth, another ferry connects Mudeford with Mudeford Beach. Operated by two boats built specifically for the service, *Josephine* and *Josephine II*, back up at busy times is provided by the *Ferry Dame*, which, as the smallest in the fleet, also takes over when business is slack. The two *Josephines* are unusual among domestic passenger vessels in that they are propelled by water jets. This makes them very manoeuvrable, giving them the ability to slide sideways through the water as well as going ahead and astern. When not engaged on the ferry, one of the boats, usually the *Josephine*, offers angling and mackerel fishing trips to sea.

The entrance to Christchurch Harbour at Mudeford is called the Run. It is very narrow here compared with the vast extent of the harbour itself, so as a result the tide can sluice along through it very quickly – so quickly that the old Board of Trade Boatmaster's Licence for Christchurch Harbour specifically forbade passage through the Run on strong ebb tides.

*Headland Pal* at Tuckton Tea Gardens.

Aboard *Headland Pal*.

*Headland Queen*.

*Headland Belle.*

Aboard *Headland Pal.*

*Wick Ferry.*

*Josephine II* leaves Mudeford.

Aboard *Josephine II*.

*Josephine* on her moorings off Mudeford.

*Ferry Dame* at Mudeford Beach.

# Chapter 4

# Western Solent

The Western Solent was a big dropping off point for passengers from excursion paddle steamers at the piers at Yarmouth, Totland Bay and, before the First World War, Alum Bay, but it was never a big picking up point. The western Isle of Wight has ever been fairly quiet, with the big concentrations of tourists at the resorts at the eastern end staying at Ryde, Sandown, Shanklin and Ventnor.

Of course, outward-bound trips were advertised and passengers did climb aboard, but not in the same numbers that landed. In the early 1960s, when I used to sail regularly aboard the paddle steamer *Embassy*, she often decanted 500 at Totland Bay around lunchtime, but collected just thirty for the return trip to Bournemouth.

Today, from Lymington, Puffin Cruises offer trips aboard two twelve-seater motor boats – *Puffin Billy* and *Black Puffin* – down the river past the marinas, which are full of yachts of all sizes. They continue onwards towards the mouth of the river and the saltgrass marshes, which are a haven for sea birds, including gulls, ducks, terns, waders and divers. *Black Puffin* is dolled up with much use of the skull and crossbones as a sort of pirate galleon, although in truth she is just an ordinary boat with a roof, above which is a stick with a bit of cloth attached to represent a galleon-style square topsail.

At Keyhaven three vessels ferry passengers down to Hurst Castle, which dates from 1544 and is one of a string of defences thrown up by Henry VIII after he had sacked the pope and the Catholic Church and set himself up as head of the newly founded Church of England. The castle is at the end of a long and narrow shingle spit connecting it to the Hampshire mainland and there is a lonely and remote feeling when you get there. It is also the perfect platform for viewing the Solent approaches and the western Isle of Wight coast down to the Needles. The service is run by the MCA-certificated *Solent Rose* and the new twelve-seater launches *Henrietta Rose* and *Victoria Rose*.

From Yarmouth you can take a trip on the *Coral Star* to view Hurst Castle or sail down the island coast to get a close up view of the Needles' rocks and lighthouse. This is a stunning trip and, for me, is one of the most scenic and enjoyable of all in this section of the south coast. I have been past the Needles countless times in my life. I am very familiar with them, but seeing them so close from a small boat puts them into a different sort of awe-inspiring perspective.

Near the top, beneath the Needles Battery, is the Victorian fort. Further east you can see cliff falls and then there is Alum Bay with its spectacular colours of sand. Saddest of all is Totland Bay Pier; now in derelict condition, it was once not only the home of the Trinity House Isle of Wight pilot cutter, but was also a main unloading point for the paddle steamers arriving from Weymouth, Swanage, Bournemouth, Southampton, Southsea and Ryde.

*Coral Star* was built for services between Torquay, Brixham and Dartmouth in 1962 and has only recently arrived at Yarmouth after a major rebuild. She is a typical open boat with some undercover accommodation and deserves everyone's support in her new role. The trip from Yarmouth to the Needles should be on everyone's to-do list.

However, if you want a shorter boat ride to see the Needles then go to Alum Bay, where Needles Pleasure Craft operate the *Ramblin' Rose* and the *Yarmouth Rose* from a small pier off the beach. The trip is about 20 minutes in length and gives close-up views of the Needles as well as fine views of the many seabirds. The company also has a fast rib to give rides with a higher thrill factor around the iconic Needles.

If you don't have a car then there is an open-top bus service from Yarmouth to Alum Bay, which is a joy in itself. The walk down to the beach is long and scenic. The walk back up is even harder, but don't worry as there is a Swiss-style ski lift to whisk you down to and up from the beach for any brave enough to try it.

*Black Puffin* at Lymington.

*Solent Rose* leaving Keyhaven.

Aboard *Solent Rose*.

Twelve-seater *Victoria Rose* between Hurst Castle and Keyhaven.

*Coral Star* at Yarmouth.

*Coral Star* at Yarmouth.

*Coral Star* off the Needles.

Totland Bay's now derelict pier.

*Yarmouth Rose.*

Alum Bay and its Swiss-style ski lift with *Ramblin' Rose* alongside the little pier.

# Chapter 5

# Southampton, Cowes and Portsmouth

Until the 1960s, excursion sailings from Southampton were dominated by Red Funnel. In their heyday you could have hopped on a paddle steamer here, which might have taken you on a local trip to Ryde or Southsea or beyond to the Isle of Wight resorts at Sandown, Shanklin, Ventnor, Totland Bay or Yarmouth. For the more adventurous, there were trips around the Isle of Wight, to Brighton in the east, Bournemouth, Swanage and Weymouth in the west and, until the Second World War, across the Channel to Cherbourg. By the 1950s decline had set in and Red Funnel's last ship capable of sailing to sea and around the Isle of Wight, *Balmoral*, made her last trip for the company in September 1968.

Meanwhile, at Southampton a fleet of small passenger vessels filled an increasing gap in the market, offering trips around the docks and making themselves available for private charters. By the 1950s they were in the hands of Horace Barkham and Bill Hog, who bought up former Gosport ferries and refurbished them for this work.

Bill had a vision for improving passenger amenities and so snapped up deckhouses that he had spotted lying on the quay at Weymouth, and which had been taken from Cosens' paddle steamers *Consul*, *Embassy* and *Emperor of India* in 1958, to fit to his vessels at Southampton to provide covered accommodation on deck.

In the 1970s Bill started to replace his elderly second-hand tonnage with new, building the *Solent Scene*, *Island Scene* and *Ocean Scene*, all of which were state-of-the-art small domestic passenger vessels capable of carrying 250 passengers that were suitable both for excursions and for the charter market. He was determined to try to improve the standards and had *Solent Scene* designed to try to maximise both on-deck and covered accommodation so that passengers would still travel and be able to see where they were going even when it was raining. He was also keen for the boats to be suited for the charter market so they were fitted with small galleys to enable hot meals to be served.

To help finance building *Solent Scene*, Bill took out a loan with interest at a fixed rate. During the building interest rates went down, so when he came to order his second boat, *Island Scene*, he opted for a variable interest rate only to find that interest rates then went up. Such are the challenges for a small domestic passenger vessel operator trying hard to do the right thing.

In the late 1980s the business, by then trading as Blue Funnel, was taken over by Mark Rayment, and today it is run by his son Lee. They have been proactive in building new tonnage not only for their Southampton operations, but also for their work out of Cowes and Portsmouth with their sister company Solent & Wightline.

However, the market has changed in recent years and dock cruises from Southampton are not as popular as they once were. Conversely, the market for short trips around Portsmouth Harbour has grown massively with the developments around the Spinnaker Tower, so the main tripping focus has moved from Southampton to Portsmouth.

The only large vessel that Blue Funnel now bases at Southampton is the *Ocean Scene*. She mostly undertakes charters but does still offer some cruises around the docks, as well as longer trips taking in the Rivers Itchen, Test and Hamble, and sometimes sailing as far as Beaulieu.

Blue Funnel acquired the Hythe ferry in 2017, which operates the 10-minute crossing between Hythe Pier and Southampton. This is one of those ferries that you wonder why it exists at all as the bus and road connections between Hythe and Southampton are really quite good, but bonkers or not it works; passengers want to travel on it and it remains popular. The main boat on the route is the *Hythe Scene*, formerly known as *Great Expectations* and at one time mainstay of the Tilbury Gravesend ferry service on the Thames. She runs every day from early in the morning to late in the evening, offering good views of whatever ships happen to be in at Southampton at any one time. Travel on her to Hythe and you have the added joy of taking the somewhat antiquated tram down Hythe Pier to the shore.

Cowes is the base for Blue Funnel's main Solent and Portsmouth operations, and this is where you may find their *Wight Scene* and *Solent Cat*, as well as *Ali Cat*, which was built in 2017 by Manor Marine at Portland for an estimated £1.6 million. These vessels offer a 2½- to 3-hour tour of Cowes and Portsmouth Harbours; a cheap day shopping trip between Cowes and Portsmouth; and Portsmouth Harbour tours from Spinnaker Quay and HMS *Warrior* at Portsmouth, sailing past the Royal Navy dockyard and the cross-Channel ferry terminal. They are also available for charter.

Between them, Blue Funnel and Solent & Wightline also field six large launches: *Jenny Ann*, *Jenny Lee*, *Jenny M*, *Jenny R*, *Jenny Blue* and *Oliver B*. They are used for harbour tours at quieter times, for school parties, as relief on the Hythe ferry, for trips from Beaulieu, connections to the Spithead forts and for charter work throughout the Solent.

The Gosport ferry has three vessels: *Spirit of Gosport*, *Spirit of Portsmouth* and *Harbour Spirit*, which was built in Croatia in 2015 and brought to the UK as deck cargo aboard the heavy lift ship *Ameonitas*.

The ferry runs from 5.30 a.m. to midnight every day and generally requires only two vessels to provide the service, with the third being available for charters as well as summer excursions. These range from Portsmouth Harbour tours through to day trips to Ryde with a train connection to Sandown, a cruise through the Solent to the Needles with time ashore at Yarmouth, to the Beaulieu River and a two-river cruise taking in both the Hamble and Medina.

For those who like sailing there are opportunities to get afloat aboard the Thames sailing barge *Alice*, which is based at Portsmouth. Built in 1954 at Wivenhoe, she can accommodate twenty guests, with sleeping accommodation also provided, and while not generally offering advertised public trips, she is available for private hire. She specialises in stag dos, hen parties and corporate work.

Based at Southampton, *Princess Carolyn* undertakes corporate charters, weddings and so on.

Between Warsash and Hamble the pink-painted *Claire* and *Emily* provide a ferry carrying twelve each.

At Cowes the chain ferry, which rejoices in the name *Floating Bridge No. 6*, provides a link across the River Medina. The vessel was new in 2017 and arrived amid much trumpeting only to encounter several serious teething problems from the outset. It was found that the vessel grounded on low water springs and the loading ramps at each end were insufficiently long, causing damage to cars as they drove on and off – oops! These issues have now been addressed and the ferry is in service once again.

*Ocean Scene.*

*Ocean Scene* off Hythe.

*Hythe Scene* arriving at Southampton's Town Quay.

Aboard *Hythe Scene*.

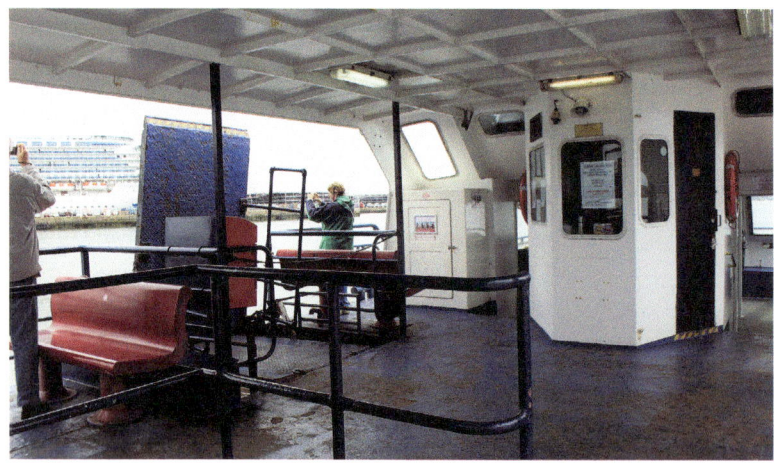

Aboard *Hythe Scene*.

*Wight Scene*.

*Wight Scene* at West Cowes.

*Solent Cat* in Portsmouth Harbour.

*Solent Cat* in Portsmouth Harbour.

That's what I like to see – crew members cleaning *Solent Cat*'s windows.

*Right*: *Ali Cat* at Portsmouth.

*Below*: *Ali Cat* passing Endeavour Quay in Gosport.

*Jenny Blue* at Southampton.

*Jenny M* at Portsmouth.

*Jenny Lee* at West Cowes.

*Jenny Ann* at Southampton.

*Harbour Spirit* approaching the Portsmouth pontoon.

*Harbour Spirit* leaving Portsmouth.

*Spirit of Gosport* at Gosport.

Aboard *Harbour Spirit*.

Aboard *Harbour Spirit* with HMS *Warrior* in the background.

Aboard *Harbour Spirit* at Gosport.

Thames sailing barge *Alice*.

*Claire*, the Hamble–Warsash ferry.

The old Cowes *Floating Bridge No. 5* on buoys at Gosport.

Cowes *Floating Bridge No. 6* in service.

# Chapter 6

# West Sussex

The Sussex coast was once the home to the paddle steamers of P&A Campbell and others. Based at Newhaven, trips were offered to sea from Brighton, Eastbourne, Hastings, Worthing and Bognor Regis as far as Folkestone in the east and the Isle of Wight in the west, with extensions sometimes being made further afield to Bournemouth. Cross-Channel trips to Boulogne were also popular before the Second World War and were revived again for the 1955/56 seasons when the requirement for passengers travelling to hold passports was relaxed.

However, the Sussex coast was never an easy place to operate seagoing excursions. When the wind blows from the west through to the east there is no shelter. The piers are exposed to the full force of the elements and it was not uncommon for steamers to have picked passengers up at, say, Brighton Pier in the morning, and to have then been unable to land them again later in the day, having to take everybody on to be put ashore at Newhaven Harbour instead.

Today all that has gone. The landing stages on the piers have been damaged and in most cases removed. The pier at Bognor Regis is no more. However, it is still possible to have a boat ride in West Sussex, although generally in calmer waters than enjoyed by the paddle steamers of yesteryear.

Working from the west to the east, let's start with the ferry across the entrance to Langstone Harbour. Operated by Baker Trayte Marine, *Pride of Hayling* connects Ferry Point on Hayling Island and Eastney Point on the Portsmouth side. The service was relaunched in 2016 at a special ceremony presided over by ballet star Wayne Sleep and the Mayor of Havant, and it operates every day throughout the year. It is not a long boat ride but I think it is worth experiencing. Hayling Island has an away from it all feeling about it and the pub overlooking the harbour entrance is an excellent vantage point from which to watch weekend sailors coming and going in and out of the harbour, as well as the occasional passing dredger.

You can also take a trip around Langstone Harbour from Ferry Point aboard the small twelve-seater *Rosie K,* which, from time to time, offers the opportunity to see parts of the harbour otherwise inaccessible from the land.

There are two boat options in Chichester Harbour. The *Wingate III* offers 1½-hour trips in the summer from Itchenor Harbour up to four times a day to allow passengers to view the multiplicity yachts and wildlife, including a wide range of seabirds. Chichester Harbour is also home to a colony of about thirty seals and *Wingate III* also offers slightly longer trips to view them, as well as being available for private parties and charters.

This boat started life as a lifeboat on the P&O liner *Canberra* and there is a picture aboard of her loaded to the gunwales with marines at Port Stanley during the Falklands Conflict in 1982. After *Canberra* was withdrawn she was saved and started her new passenger carrying career initially at Arbroath before moving to Chichester in 1998.

Also running short trips to view Chichester Harbour's wildlife and scenery is the *Solar Heritage*, which picks up at Emsworth and sometimes at Itchenor and is owned by the Harbour Authority. She is an Aquabus C60 – a pollution-free, solar-powered catamaran that can reach 11 knots while carrying sixty passengers, although in the harbour she carries just fifty and her speed is restricted to 8 knots.

*Solar Heritage* began life as one of three solar-powered ferries operating out of Neuchatel in Switzerland's Three Lakes Region (Les Trois Lacs), the area that hosted the Swiss 2002 National Exposition devoted to nature and technology. The three ferries carried people to and from one of the exhibitions in the middle of the lake on a continuous basis for six months between May and October 2002. The exhibition hosting the solar ferries was devoted to alternative energy, and part of the reason for obtaining a solar-powered boat by Chichester Harbour Conservancy was to heighten local awareness and interest in these matters. The vessel has two sources of power – electromagnetic energy from the sun and conventional electricity from the National Grid.

*Solar Heritage* arrived in Itchenor in May 2004 after a 24-hour drive across Europe on three articulated lorries and was reconstructed at Northshore Ltd by her Swiss engineers, who were brought over especially for the occasion. The benefits of using an electrically driven solar-powered catamaran as opposed to more conventional fuel are that the vessel is silent and therefore causes no disturbance to birds, animals or humans. There are no exhaust and carbon dioxide emissions, and there is virtually no wash as a result of the twin hull configuration, which reduces salt marsh and estuary bank erosion.

Another option to get afloat at Chichester is on one of the Chichester Canal Trust's two narrowboats, *Kingfisher* and *Richmond*. They offer 75-minute trips along the canal between the basin at Chichester and Donnington – a beautiful stretch with excellent views and prolific wildlife. Also scheduled are special fish and chip and cream tea cruises. The canal was opened in 1823 and was intended as part of a through inland route for barges from Portsmouth to London, but it was never a commercial success as it was cheaper to carry the cargos by sea instead.

Brighton West Pier is a wreck. Brighton Palace Pier is still very much open for a funfair sort of experience but its landing stages for boats to pick up passengers are long gone. However, you can still take a sea trip from Brighton if you take yourself along to the Marina, which is home to Brighton Marina Watertours and their four boats, *Rossann*, *Voyager*, *Thresher* and *Adept*, as well as their rib, which offers all the thrills of a high-speed whizz crashing through the waves out to sea.

Between them the boats offer 45-minute coastal cruises and 2-hour trips around the Rampton Windfarm, as well as mackerel fishing trips. They are available for private hire and specialise in hen and stag parties, but they also find a use as workboats in connection with the windfarm.

They are a far cry from the glorious Brighton paddle steamers of yesteryear with names to conjure with like *Brighton Belle* (which gets a mention in Graham Green's novel *Brighton Rock*), *Ravenswood* and *Glen Gower*, but these small modern-day Brighton craft are still boats and they do take passengers to sea. You can once again see this part of the Sussex coast from the sea and for that we should all be very grateful. The hen and stag parties are not exactly my cup of tea, but a 45-minute coastal cruise or a 2-hour run around the windfarm? I'll buy a ticket for them any day.

*Pride of Hayling* crossing the entrance of Langstone Harbour.

*Pride of Hayling* alongside at Ferry Point.

*Pride of Hayling* at Ferry Point with *Rosie K* ahead of her.

*Kingfisher* on the Chichester Canal.

*Richmond* in Chichester's canal basin.

Chichester Canal crew fire training.

*Wingate III* in Chichester Harbour.

*Wingate III* arrives at Itchenor.

*Wingate III.*

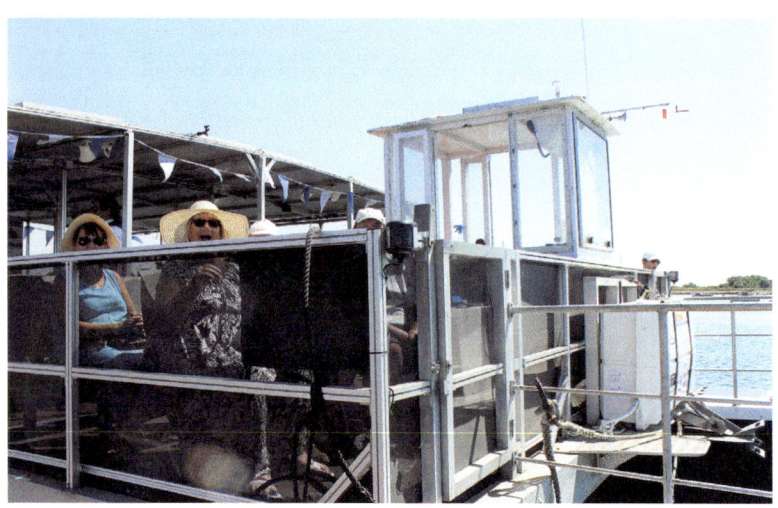

*Solar Heritage* at Emsworth.

*Solar Heritage* loading for a trip around Chichester Harbour.

*Solar Heritage.*

*Rossann* at Brighton Marina.

*Adept* and Brighton Marina Water Tours' RIB at Brighton Marina.

All aboard for a 45-minute trip to sea on *Rossann*.

*Rossann* sets off from Brighton Marina.

# Chapter 7

# Isle of Wight Ferries

The oldest company still operating to the Isle of Wight is Red Funnel, which has its origins in 1820 when George Ward and William Fitzhugh set up a ferry service between Cowes and Southampton. The business was incorporated as the Southampton, Isle of Wight & South of England Royal Mail Steam Packet Company Ltd (which is better known today under its trading name of Red Funnel) in 1861.

Not only did the company run this ferry, but it also expanded into operating excursion steamers to the Isle of Wight and beyond from the now derelict Royal Pier. From 1885 they added tug ownership to their portfolio, becoming one of Southampton's two main tug operators servicing the great ocean liners and cargo ships that visited the port.

Red Funnel was in the forefront of building new paddle steamers for the Southampton to Cowes ferry service from the 1880s, and as cars started to come on line a few were accommodated on the foredecks of their steamers, having been driven aboard over pontoons at the same level as the ships' decks.

The company was also quick to implement new technology with their first diesel-powered vessel, *Medina*, being built in 1931. Seven years later they built *Vecta* with the then very novel Voith Schneider propulsion units, which can push a ship in any direction and are today standard on many ferries worldwide.

In 1947 they acquired a former tank landing craft, which they renamed *Norris Castle*. They converted her into their first ship that could accommodate a large number of cars and lorries, which were driven aboard through a bow door. She was followed in 1959 by the purpose-built drive-on ferry *Carisbrooke Castle*. Three similar vessels were also added to the fleet: *Osborne Castle*, *Cowes Castle* and a new *Norris Castle* in the 1960s.

Drive through facilities were designed into the next addition to the fleet, *Netley Castle*, in 1974 and she was such a success that *Cowes Castle* and *Norris Castle* were enlarged and fitted with both bow and stern doors as well. They continued in service until the new generation of ships arrived on the scene in the mid-1990s, with *Red Falcon*, *Red Osprey* and *Red Eagle* continuing in service today. They provide good quality passenger accommodation and, because of the length of the crossing, which takes about an hour, they also provide meals, including fish and chips, curries and a pasta dish.

In February 2018 Red Funnel placed a £10 million order for a new ro-ro freight ferry from UK shipbuilder Cammell Laird to join the route. The new ship is designed to provide additional year-round freight capacity for the service which currently handles 53 per cent of all freight movements across the Solent. At 74 metres in length, she will provide 265 lane metres of roll-on roll-off freight capacity and will carry up to twelve passengers. To minimise the environmental footprint, the hull shape has been designed specifically to reduce wash and a propulsion package has been selected to make her highly fuel efficient while meeting the latest Tier III emission regulations. The use of azimuth thrusters supplied by Rolls-Royce will also make the ship very manoeuvrable. The crossing time will be identical to Red Funnel's existing Raptor Class ro-ro passenger ships and she will use the same berths in Southampton and East Cowes. The new ship is scheduled to be delivered in the spring of 2019.

Red Funnel first introduced a high-speed service between Southampton and Cowes in 1933 with their small *Island Enterprise,* which was capable of 30 knots. She reduced the journey time to just 35 minutes but this service was not revived after the war. Following the challenge of possible competition from hovercraft, they bought their first hydrofoil, *Shearwater,* in 1968 and have maintained a fast connection ever since. Currently the service is operated by *Red Jets 3, 4, 6* and *7*.

The Wightlink services between Lymington and Yarmouth, Portsmouth and Fishbourne and Portsmouth and Ryde all have their origins in the railways. The first Lymington to Yarmouth service started in 1850 and was run by the steamer *Solent*. The London & South Western Railway took over the route in 1884 using three small paddle steamers, which extended the journey on to Totland Bay and Alum Bay in the summers until 1927. Also in 1927, another more modern paddle steamer, *Freshwater,* was added to the fleet. Surviving until 1959, she then had a short career sailing on the Sussex coast in 1960 and from Swanage and Bournemouth in 1961.

Before the arrival of the first purpose-built drive-on drive-off Voith Schneider-propelled car ferry, *Lymington,* in 1939, cars were transported on towboats. These were essentially small barges onto which the cars were driven before being towed by a paddle steamer across the Solent.

After the Second World War the Southern Railway wanted to build another Voith Schneider-propelled ferry but were thwarted in this as the German factory making the machinery had been heavily bombed by the British in the war. Instead they built the *Farringford* in 1948, which was propelled by independently operating paddle wheels. In 1959 a new Voith Schneider-propelled *Freshwater* replaced the paddler of the same name.

The larger *Cenwulf* and *Cenred* took over the service in 1973 and they were joined by the *Caedmon*, transferred from Portsmouth in 1984, with the three continuing until the present fleet of *Wight Sun, Wight Sky* and *Wight Light* arrived in 2008. At 1,500 GRT they are considerably larger than their predecessors and caused controversy at Lymington, with environmental enthusiasts complaining that they would damage wildlife habitats and destroy the salt marshes. The dispute rumbled on for some years but is now resolved, with the ferries making their slow and stately procession up and down the Lymington River at only a very modest speed. The basic service today needs only two ships, although a third is held in reserve in case of necessity.

Ryde Pier first opened in 1814 and was extended several times during the nineteenth century. A separate tramway pier was constructed in 1864 and a new railway pier right next to it opened in 1880 – the same year that the London & South Western Railway and the London, Brighton & South Coast Railway jointly bought up the existing small fleet of paddle steamers that ran between Portsmouth and Ryde.

In the ensuing years they gradually improved the fleet, building a number of new paddle steamers in the 1890s and in the run up to the First World War. In the 1930s four new, modern and much larger paddle steamers, *Southsea*, *Whippingham*, *Sandown* and *Ryde*, were added to the fleet. After the Second World War, the diesel-powered *Brading*, *Southsea* and *Shanklin* arrived and started to knock the paddlers off their perches.

The railway connection disappeared in 1984 with privatisation, since which time the Portsmouth to Ryde route has been operated by fast catamarans. Today the *Wight Ryder I* and *Wight Ryder II* provide the service, taking just 20 minutes each way for the crossing.

As at Lymington, tow boats were used to carry vehicles between the Portsmouth Harbour slipway and Fishbourne from as early as the 1860s. The first drive-on drive-off car ferries designed for the route, *Fishbourne*, *Wooton* and *Hilsea*, were built in the late 1920s and continued in service until replaced by the larger *Fishbourne* and *Camber Queen* in 1961. The first of the C Class car ferries, *Cuthred*, arrived on the scene in 1969, and with *Caedmon*, delivered in 1973, they maintained the service until the even larger Saint Class ships were built in the 1980s.

Today the service is maintained by the *St Cecilia*, *St Faith*, *St Clare* and the brand new *Victoria of Wight*, which arrived in August 2018. At over 8,041 GRT, she is a seriously large Isle of Wight ferry. Built in Turkey as part of a £45 million investment program in both the ships and the terminals to enhance customer experience, *Victoria of Wight* is a hybrid energy ship that uses a combination of battery power and conventional engines. She therefore links Portsmouth and Fishbourne with minimal emissions and more quietly than the rest of the fleet. She can carry 178 cars and more than a thousand passengers.

Hovercraft were once seen as a new dawn for ferry operations, but they never really caught on and the only passenger route currently operating them in the UK is between the beaches at Southsea and Ryde. In 1962 the world's first all-metal hovercraft, *SR.N1*, ran trials on this route, but it was not until 1964 that a regular service was started. Today it is operated by the *Solent Flyer* and *Island Flyer*, both built in 2016 as part of a £10 million investment program.

Southampton's derelict Royal Pier, from which Red Funnel's excursions once ran.

Red Funnel's first Southampton ro-ro terminal is now derelict.

*Red Eagle* arriving at Southampton.

*Red Falcon* in Southampton Water.

*Red Osprey* off Netley

Aboard *Red Eagle*, leaving Southampton.

Aboard *Red Eagle* off Cowes.

Aboard *Red Eagle*, approaching the East Cowes terminal.

One of *Red Eagle*'s comfortable saloons.

*Red Eagle*'s hot food servery – yum, yum!

*Red Jet 4* crossing Cowes to Southampton.

*Red Jet 6* at Southampton.

*Red Jet 7* leaving Southampton.

*Red Jet 7* unusually berthed at East Cowes.

*Wight Sky* crossing from Yarmouth to Lymington.

*Wight Sun* in reserve at Portsmouth.

Aboard *Wight Light* between Lymington and Yarmouth.

*Wight Light*'s emergency rescue boat.

A life-raft pod on *Wight Light*. This can be activated from the bridge by a vacuum pump.

*Left*: What a lot of two-tier lights. From top down: all round white anchor light; higher white steaming light; and lower white steaming light. All round red, white and red lights mean 'I'm restricted in my ability to manoeuvre', while just two reds means 'Not under command'.

*Below*: Part of *Wight Light*'s saloon accommodation.

*Wight Ryder 1* alongside Portsmouth Harbour station.

*Wight Ryder 1* crossing from Portsmouth to Ryde.

*Wight Ryder 1* returning to Portsmouth.

*Wight Ryder 2* off Gosport.

*St Faith* leaving Portsmouth.

*St Faith* leaving Fishbourne.

*St Cecelia* arriving at Portsmouth.

*St Clare* off Southsea.

*St Clare* approaching Portsmouth.

*Victoria of Wight* leaving Portsmouth.

Boarding *St Cecilia* at Portsmouth.

*St Cecilia*'s life-raft pods, which are all capable of being activated from the bridge.

*St Cecilia*'s fast rescue boat.

One of *St Cecilia*'s passenger saloons.

*St Clare*'s bridge.

One of *St Clare*'s passenger saloons.

Approaching the Portsmouth terminal on *St Clare*.

Vacuum mooring for Wightlink's Portsmouth to Fishbourne route: suckers stick to the ship's side to hold her in place without the need for ropes.

*Solent Flyer* off Southsea.

*Solent Flyer* glides up Southsea Beach.

*Solent Flyer*: engines off, skirt down.

# Chapter 8

# Cross-Channel Ferries

Cross-Channel ferries have changed so much in my lifetime. When I was a boy in the 1950s, there were no drive-on car ferries at all on this section of the south coast. The mail boats did carry cars, but they were driven onto netting, which was then lifted up by cranes to be deposited in the ship's hold.

Every cross-Channel ferry in this area was run by the railways in those days, with timetabled rail connections at each end. When I say the railways I really mean British Railways, which controlled almost everything, although the French SNCF did have a toehold on the Newhaven–Dieppe route.

The London & South Western Railway were in the forefront of attempts to operate cross-Channel ferries from Southampton. They received parliamentary approval for this in 1849 and by 1851 services were being offered to France and the Channel Islands under their name. They were also the first to start the process of getting rid of paddle steamers and replacing them with propeller-driven ships.

Along the coast at Weymouth, the Great Western Railway had an involvement in the services to the Channel Islands from the 1860s, but it was not until 1889 that they took over the route in their own right. In the ensuing two decades, with new steamers built for the Southampton and Weymouth companies, competition became fierce when racing to be the first to reach St Helier in Jersey was commonplace. This ended on 16 April 1897 when the GWR's *Ibex* tried to get ahead of the LSWR's *Frederica* by taking the inside passage off Corbiere but misjudged her position, striking the Normontaise Rock, losing one of her propeller blades and putting a hole in her bottom in the process.

This is a good reminder of the dangers of the Channel Islands and Brittany coasts. They have a huge tidal range of more than 45 feet. There are very fast tidal currents and vast numbers of offshore rocky outcrops, many of which disappear for much of the tidal cycle, lurking just beneath the surface ready to skewer the mariner whose navigational calculations are not exactly spot on.

In the days before radar and satellite navigation largely solved this problem, Channel Island ferries did run aground from time to time, sometimes with dramatic effect. There is a photograph of the GWR's *Roebuck* perched in the cleft of a rock with the water far below her as the tide has run away. And she was not alone; a number of railway steamers came to grief in fog on Channel Island rocks, including the brand-new *St Patrick* on 5 August 1932 when she ripped a hole in her bottom off Corbiere in thick fog, causing serious damage to her hull. Fortunately she didn't sink and was towed to St Helier.

During the 1950s the Southampton to Le Havre service was in the hands of the *Normania*, built in 1952, with the St Malo connection being taken by the *Falaise* of 1947. These were overnight routes with the steamers sailing out one night, spending the day in the French ports and returning the following night.

In 1961 the Southampton to Channel Islands route was closed, with all sailings being concentrated on Weymouth. By 1964 British Railways retrenched further, closing the Le Havre and St Malo routes, which they claimed were unprofitable, and earmarked their *Normannia* and *Falaise* for conversion into car ferries for Dover and Newhaven instead.

With the closure of these services, the Norwegian company Thoresen Ferries stepped into the gap in the market, making a huge success of a new Southampton to Cherbourg connection using the brand new ro-ro ship *Viking I*, which looked of space age design when compared with the old railway boats she replaced.

The railways continued to be slow to catch up. As late as 1972, British Rail, under their Sealink brand, were still transporting cars to the Channel Islands. These were craned aboard their cargo ship *Moose*, which accompanied the mail boat on the crossing on which their owners travelled. But progress was at last at hand. For 1973 the *Falaise* was brought from Newhaven to inaugurate the first drive-on ferry from Weymouth to the Channel Islands. By 1977 services were provided by two ro-ro ferries from Weymouth, *Earl Godwin* and *Caledonian Princess*, and one from Portsmouth, *Earl William*.

It was the start of the retreat of the railway in the 1960s that opened the door for new operators, and one that has lasted longest is Condor, which started up a hydrofoil service between St Helier and St Malo in 1964. I recall looking at these little craft back then and wondering if they were man enough for the sometimes tumultuous Channel Island waters, but I was wrong; it is not always rough there and the service proved to be a great success.

Condor took advantage of the chaos in the final denouement of conventional ro-ro ferries of Sealink and British Channel Island Ferries in 1987, making their first connection to the UK that year with their *Condor 7*. Since then, and in association with Commodore Shipping, they have come to dominate the UK to Channel Island market and now have four vessels: *Commodore Clipper* (a conventional ro-ro ferry that makes one round trip a day to the Islands from Portsmouth), *Commodore Goodwill* (which carries freight only), *Condor Liberation* (a high-speed craft that runs between Poole and the Channel Islands) and *Condor Rapide* (a fast catamaran that connects the Channel Islands and France).

As the railway influence on cross-Channel work declined, other operators appeared, but it is Brittany Ferries that has grown ever stronger and which now controls the market. Founded in 1972 by Alexis Gourvennec and a group of fellow Breton farmers wanting to export their cauliflowers and artichokes to the UK, Brittany Ferries built their first ship, *Penn-Ar-Bed*, in 1974 and in 1976 started operating between St Malo and Portsmouth.

In the mid-1980s they acquired the Truckline Ferries service from Poole to Cherbourg and tried to muscle in on the Channel Islands market with British Channel Island Ferries, although that was not a success. Indeed, the early days were not without their difficulties, with two vessels running aground in St Malo, three ships being plagued with engine problems, and trade union strikes and fishermen's disputes causing the closure of ports.

In 1989 they built the *Bretagne*, which provided new levels of luxury in ferry travel and currently runs between Portsmouth and St Malo. She was followed in the next couple of decades by a succession of top class ferries including *Amorique* (Plymouth–Roscoff), *Barfleur* (Poole–Cherbourg), *Cap Finistere* (Portsmouth–Spain), *Contentin* (freight only Poole–Cherbourg), *Etretat* (no frills Portsmouth–Le Havre), *Mont St Michel* (Portsmouth–Caen), *Normandie* (Portsmouth–Caen), *Normandie Express* (high-speed Portsmouth–Cherbourg) and *Port Aven* (Plymouth–Roscoff, Spain and Cork).

A new ship, *Honfleur*, has been ordered for 2019. She is set to be powered by liquid natural gas and will be 42,000 GRT. All this is a far cry from the old and, by modern standards, tiny *Falaise* of just 3,700 GRT, aboard which British Cold War spies Guy Burgess and Donald Maclean escaped from Southampton to St Malo on 25 May 1951.

Along the coast at Newhaven, the London, Brighton & South Coast Railway started rail-connected services to Dieppe in 1862. Although they built their first propeller-driven ship in 1893, they continued to operate paddle steamers on the route almost up to the First World War, with their paddle steamer *Paris,* built in 1888, not being withdrawn until 1912.

In the interwar years, now in the hands of the Southern Railway, and after the war, with British Railways, the key thing on this route was speed so as to try to keep the voyage time to a minimum. Unlike between Dover and Calais, which has an easy crossing time of

*Commodore Clipper* at Portsmouth.

about an hour and a half, or Southampton to Le Havre or St Malo, which is long enough for passengers to sleep their way across, Newhaven to Dieppe was in-between, being, at over 4 hours, too long a trip for the impatient traveller and too short for passengers to get their heads down. A succession of fast ships were therefore built for the route to try to address this issue, including the *Brighton, Londres, Arromanche* and *Lisieux,* which could all crack on at up to 24 knots, about 6 knots faster than most other cross-Channel ferries elsewhere, thereby shaving as much as an hour off the crossing time.

The first drive-on car ferry came to Newhaven in 1964 with the arrival of the newly converted *Falaise* from Southampton. The purpose-built *Senlac* was delivered in 1974 and she lasted in partnership with various French ferries, particularly *Villandry* and *Valencay,* until 1987, by which time the railway ownership had been sold off.

Since then the Newhaven – Dieppe crossing has rather been the Cinderella of cross-Channel ferry services, with various operators trying their luck, including P&O Stena, Hoverspeed and LD Lines. Today the service is run by sister ships *Côte d'Albâtre* and *Seven Sisters,* which were built in 2005 and 2006 respectively for Transmanche Ferries, which is an offshoot of the large Danish operator DFDS. The onboard facilities include a lounge with magnificent panoramic windows with sea views, a bar, restaurant, shop and a children's play area. There are also quiet lounges where you can relax and sleep, plus spacious outdoor decks and fifty en suite cabins.

*Condor Liberation* leaving Poole Harbour.

*Condor Rapide* leaving St Malo.

*Barfleur* leaving Poole Harbour.

*Cap Finistere.*

*Etretat.*

*Mont St Michel.*

*Normandie.*

*Normandie Express* at the Portsmouth Harbour ferry terminal.

*Bretagne* loading at St Malo.

*Bretagne* at St Malo.

*Bretagne*'s deck marked out for landing a helicopter.

*Bretagne* has plenty of deck space for passengers.

*Bretagne*'s large SOLAS life rafts and rescue boat.

Aboard *Bretagne*. Remember the days when ferries had open bridge wings?

Aboard *Bretagne*. The English Channel isn't often as blue or as smooth as this.

Le Café aboard *Bretagne*.

Self-service servery aboard *Bretagne*.

*Bretagne*'s dining saloon.

*Cote D'Albatre* at Newhaven.

# Chapter 9

# Operational Preserved Steamships

Based at Southampton, *Shieldhall* is one of Britain's greatest steamship preservation success stories. Whoever would have thought back in 1988 when she was purchased for just £20,000 from Southern Water that she would still be going strong thirty years later. Everything seemed to be against her. At 268 feet in length and with a GRT of 1,753 tons, she is huge for operational preservation. However, could a ship of such size be manned and operated successfully? More to the point, how could she possibly ever be financially viable? But her owners, the Solent Steam Packet Company, which is an industrial and provident society, have proved that it can be done, and can be done so successfully.

The business model has been to run *Shieldhall* on Maritime and Coastguard Agency Class V and VI passenger certificates, which allow her to steam within the Solent and for limited coastal excursions. This keeps her outside of the full force, complexity and implementation costs of the seagoing requirements for Class III long coastal excursions. She is manned entirely by volunteers, with key personnel holding the necessary MCA certificates and donating their services but with the ability to train others for lesser roles in-house.

Built in 1955 to take Glasgow's treated sewage out to be dumped in the lower Clyde, *Shieldhall* always had passenger certificates to take eighty on her trips down the Clyde. She was withdrawn in 1976 and sold to Southern Water to fulfil a similar role dropping Southampton's sewage off the Isle of Wight until 1985.

Today *Shieldhall* offers a range of cruises each summer from Southampton within the Solent and along the Isle of Wight coast and generally makes an annual excursion to Poole. Sailing aboard her is a real delight. The number of passengers she is certificated to carry is small in comparison with her size so she seems empty even when she is full. You can visit the engine room to see the two huge vertical, triple-expansion steam engines working, visit the bridge or just sit on deck and soak up the atmosphere of sailing aboard a ship from a bygone age.

Built in 1947 for the London & North Eastern Railway's Clyde ferry services and excursions, *Waverley* spent more than a quarter of a century running on the Clyde routes to Arrochar, through the Kyles of Bute and sometimes further afield to Campbeltown from her base at Craigendoran, as well as taking her turn on the ferry services connecting

Gourock, Dunoon, Wemyss Bay and Rothesay. The last Clyde paddler to be withdrawn, *Waverley* was sold into preservation for the price of £1, since which time she has extended her scope of activities nationwide.

She has a very different business model from *Shieldhall*, spending most of the summer on the Clyde before taking off south to run excursions from Liverpool along the coast of north Wales, on the Bristol Channel, the south coast between Weymouth and the east of the Isle of Wight and then on the Thames in an area bounded by Tower Pier, Margate and Harwich. She has full MCA Class III passenger certificates for long coastal excursions and a full-time crew, and is therefore massively expensive to operate. Where *Shieldhall* gets by on an annual turnover of little more than £100,000, *Waverley's* operating costs mean that she needs to turn over approaching £2 million a year to stay solvent.

There is one other little steamship, *Monarch*, which is based at Wareham and runs short cruises along the reed-lined banks of the River Frome. She is the brainchild of Brian Waters, who conceived building her in 1984 at Chatham. Eventually completed in 2003, she first ran on the River Stour in Kent, then on the River Medina on the Isle of Wight before moving to Wareham in 2012. At 47 feet in length, she can carry just twelve passengers.

*Shieldhall* at Poole.

*Above*: *Shieldhall* at Poole.

*Right*: *Shieldhall*'s funnel.

*Shieldhall*'s windlass.

On deck aboard *Shieldhall*.

*Shieldhall*'s starboard shelter deck looking aft.

*Shieldhall*'s port shelter deck looking forwards.

*Shieldhall*'s saloon.

*Shieldhall*'s boatswain's locker.

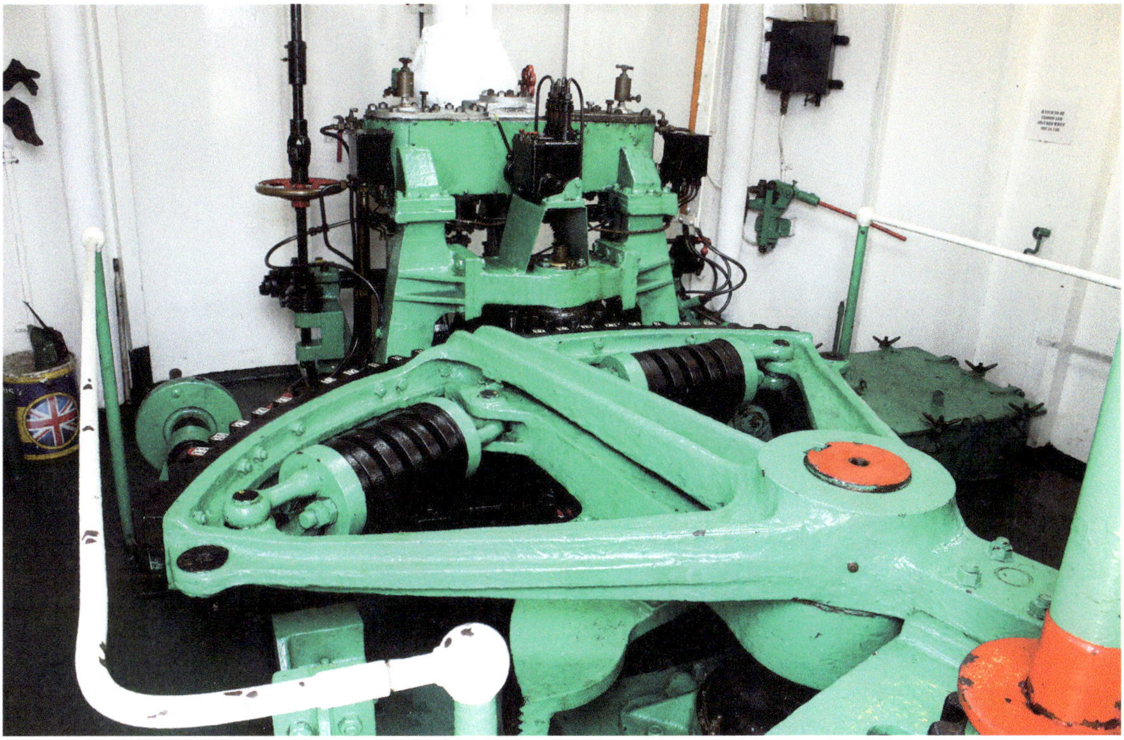

*Above*: *Shieldhall*'s steam steering engine.

*Right*: *Shieldhall*'s port bridge telegraph.

*Shieldhall*'s engine room.

*Waverley* backing out from Swanage.

*Waverley* arriving at Swanage.

Full astern.

*Waverley.*

The docking telegraph rings: 'Heave away on the aft capstan'.

# Operational Preserved Steamships

Slow astern on the engine room telegraph.

*Waverley*'s dining saloon.

*Waverley*'s port engine room alleyway looking forwards.

*Waverley*'s engine room.

*Monarch* at Wareham.

# Vessels that can Carry more than Twelve Passengers

| Name | Built | GRT | Length | Passengers |
|---|---|---|---|---|
| *Ali Cat* | 2017 | 70 | 19.1 | 300 |
| *Alice* | 1954 | 57 | 23.5 | 20 |
| *Amorique* | 2009 | 29,468 | 167 | 1,500 |
| *Barfleur* | 1992 | 20,133 | 157.7 | 1,212 |
| *Bramble Bush Bay* | 1993 | 125 | 78.6 | n/a |
| *Bretagne* | 1989 | 25,015 | 152.8 | 2,056 |
| *Brownsea Enterprise* | 1974 | 8 | 9.7 | 37 |
| *Castello* | 1964 | 7 | 8 | 20 |
| *Cap Finistere* | 2001 | 32,728 | 203.9 | 790 |
| *Commodore Clipper* | 1999 | 13,460 | 129.1 | 500 |
| *Condor Liberation* | 2010 | 6,231 | 102 | 1,165 |
| *Condor Rapide* | 1997 | 5,007 | 86.5 | 800 |
| *Coral Star* | 1962 | 13 | 12.8 | 63 |
| *Dorset Queen* | 1938 | 33 | 17.4 | 100 |
| *Enchantress* | 1941 | 10 | 11 | 41 |
| *Etretat* | 2008 | 26,904 | 186.5 | 375 |
| *Ferry Dame* | 1989 | 8 | 9.1 | 48 |
| *Floating Bridge No. 6* | 2017 | 201 | 37 | n/a |
| *Harbour Spirit* | 2015 | 293 | 32.9 | 300 |
| *Headland Belle* | 1934 | 8 | 11 | 50 |
| *Headland Maid* | 1935 | 8 | 11 | 50 |
| *Headland Pal* | 1934 | 8 | 11 | 50 |
| *Headland Queen* | 1934 | 8 | 11 | 50 |
| *Hythe Scene* | 1992 | 68 | 21.3 | 162 |
| *Island Flyer* | 2016 | 40 | 22.4 | 80 |
| *Island Scene* | 2001 | 49 | 18.3 | 127 |
| *Jenny Ann* | 1981 | 8 | 11.6 | 59 |
| *Jenny Blue* | 1993 | 12 | 13.7 | 70 |
| *Jenny Lee* | 1985 | 12 | 13.7 | 86 |
| *Jenny M* | 1988 | 18 | 16.8 | 116 |
| *Jenny R* | 1984 | 12 | 13.7 | 86 |

| Name | Built | GRT | Length | Passengers |
|---|---|---|---|---|
| *Josephine* | 1997 | 10 | 10.7 | 86 |
| *Josephine II* | 2013 | 10 | 10.7 | 86 |
| *Kingfisher* | 2016 | 12 | 12.1 | 22 |
| *Maid of Poole* | 1999 | 50 | 25.9 | 186 |
| *Maid of the Harbour* | 2001 | 50 | 25.9 | 186 |
| *Maid of the Islands* | 1989 | 38 | 15.2 | 130 |
| *Maid of the Lakelands* | 1991 | 45 | 18.3 | 143 |
| *Mont St Michel* | 2002 | 35,592 | 173.4 | 2,200 |
| *My Girl* | 1931 | 12 | 12.2 | 52 |
| *Normandie* | 1992 | 27,541 | 151.4 | 2,123 |
| *Normandie Express* | 2000 | 6,581 | 98 | 900 |
| *Ocean Scene* | 1994 | 279 | 29 | 350 |
| *Oliver B* | 1988 | 21 | 12.2 | 72 |
| *Pont Aven* | 2004 | 41,748 | 184.6 | 2,400 |
| *Pride of Hayling* | 1989 | 15 | 11.9 | 64 |
| *Princess Caroline* | 1983 | 213 | 30.1 | 130 |
| *Purbeck Gem* | 1988 | 40 | 16.8 | 150 |
| *Purbeck Pride* | 1990 | 45 | 19.5 | 157 |
| *Purbeck Princess* | 1999 | 58 | 19.5 | 179 |
| *Ramblin' Rose* | 1988 | 35 | 15.2 | 94 |
| *Red Eagle* | 1996 | 4,075 | 93 | 896 |
| *Red Falcon* | 1994 | 4,128 | 93 | 892 |
| *Red Jet 3* | 1998 | 213 | 32 | 173 |
| *Red Jet 4* | 2003 | 342 | 39 | 271 |
| *Red Jet 6* | 2016 | 363 | 41.1 | 275 |
| *Red Jet 7* | 2018 | 363 | 41.1 | 277 |
| *Red Osprey* | 1994 | 3,953 | 93 | 896 |
| *Richmond* | 2004 | 35 | 15.2 | 40 |
| *Rossann* | 2009 | 18 | 13 | 62 |
| *Shieldhall* | 1955 | 1,753 | 81.7 | 200 |
| *Solar Heritage* | 2000 | 15 | 14.9 | 50 |
| *Solent Cat* | 2000 | 74 | 20.1 | 250 |
| *Solent Flyer* | 2016 | 40 | 22.4 | 80 |
| *Solent Scene* | 1974 | 131 | 27.4 | 213 |
| *Solent Rose* | 1968 | 22 | 14.3 | 94 |
| *Spirit of Gosport* | 2001 | 300 | 36.2 | 300 |
| *Spirit of Portsmouth* | 2005 | 377 | 36.2 | 300 |
| *St Cecelia* | 1987 | 2,968 | 77 | 722 |
| *St Clare* | 2001 | 5,359 | 87 | 878 |
| *St Faith* | 1990 | 3,009 | 77 | 722 |
| *Thresher* | 1990 | 12 | 10.7 | 28 |
| *Victoria of Wight* | 2018 | 8,041 | 89.7 | 1,170 |
| *Voyager* | 2009 | 15 | 10 | 50 |

| | | | | |
|---|---|---|---|---|
| Waverley | 1947 | 693 | 73.1 | 800 |
| Wight Light | 2008 | 2,546 | 62.4 | 359 |
| Wight Ryde I | 2009 | 520 | 40.9 | 260 |
| Wight Ryder II | 2009 | 520 | 40.9 | 260 |
| Wight Scene | 1992 | 279 | 29 | 500 |
| Wight Sky | 2008 | 2,546 | 62.4 | 359 |
| Wight Sun | 2008 | 2,546 | 62.4 | 359 |
| Wingate III | 1975 | 14 | 11 | 52 |
| Yarmouth Rose | 2013 | 35 | 15.3 | 87 |

# Acknowledgements

Pictures of Blue Funnel boats are courtesy of Lee Rayment. All other pictures are by the author.

## Also by the Author

*British Paddle Steamers – The Heyday of Excursions and Day Trips*
*Weymouth and Portland in 50 Buildings*
*PS Kingswear Castle – A Personal Tribute*
*50 Gems of Dorset*
*British Paddle Steamers – The Twilight Years*